He Was
Dying
Inside of Me

Craig T. Robinson, Jr.

Craig T. Robinson, Jr.

First Edition

Author's Note: The characters and events in this book are real.

ISBN-13: 9781453891339
ISBN-10: 1453891331

Printed in the United States of America
10 9 8 7 6 5 4 3 2 1

Consultant/Mentor/Author:

The Write Message: Karla Denise Baker

FOREWORD
by
KARLA DENISE BAKER,
Author of *Does God Have Toys in Heaven?*

As a single mother, there was no handbook on how to *raise a child after you bury a child*. Which will be my next book entitled: *HOW DO YOU RAISE A CHILD, AFTER YOU BURY A CHILD?* And if there was, I was oblivious of the fact.

I often wondered, is it possible that subconsciously I wasn't there? Is it possible that I was absent from my body, my mind, and my soul after burying my youngest son? Is it possible that I was functioning in an every day manner to those in my presence? I say yes. But behind closed doors I was a train wreck. Me being the mother of child who died before me is a weight that has not been lifted off of my heart. Every day I carry the weight around like tons of bricks, and so does my only son, Craig. All I can say is that I remember, just as he remembers. It is not easy letting go, but I found that writing helped me soothe the anguish that still resides inside of me. And now, so does my son.

I tried my best to love Craig even more after Anthony died. And as I recall, I was most overprotected of him. I had to play both roles as a parent because of the absence of his father. With me trying to step in his shoes, pants, and shirts, the shoes didn't fit me. The pants didn't fit me, nor did the shirts. I was his mother, not his father. Yet, in his eyes I became both. And somewhere in the midst of it all I began to believe that I could be both. I felt obligated to at least try. Craig was in dire need of a masculine figure to look up to. Though I was not masculine, the responsibilities of raising him as a single mother were bestowed upon my shoulders. Disappointment led to me trying to play both roles too. I didn't want him to be further disappointed. Had I thought rationally about this, at that particular time I would've realized that I could never fill those shoes, pants, and shirts. I was not born with a penis. I could not play this role of dad or father or father figure. All that I could do was hope and pray that the man whom was his father would step-up to the plate and be his father.

In a compromising position as this, you do what is needed, expected, and required to overcome the loss, the pain, the grief...and you try with all of your might to rebuild the house that had engulfed in flames. You grab a hold of the hose and you douse the fire with water, put the fire out, and then you demolish the remains, and then you utilize the blueprint (the structure) hoping to be a better parent the second go-around.

—Karla Denise Baker

To live is to suffer, to survive is me...

In 1997, I had written a poem at school that was entered in the Paterson Schools Poetry Contest called "Street Signs" Poems by the Young People of Paterson. I won Honorable Mention for my poem: **My Room**.

I miss my brother he is a flying bee.
I miss my brother, I miss him so.
He was as light and bright as snow.

I miss my brother I see the sky.
I thought that he would never die.
I miss my brother, I wish he was alive.

When I go in my room, he is alive.
When I go in my room, I can see his face.
When I go in my room, it's our place.

When I go in my room, I can hear his steps.
He is still in my heart, when I go in my room.

(Age 10)

He Was Dying Inside of Me

Craig T. Robinson, Jr.

My name is Craig, and as a nine-year-old boy I had to become a "man", because my household required one. This is when all hell broke loose in my life. This was a road I never thought I'd have to travel. This day my life would never be the same again.

Listen, ya'll don't expect too much from me because for (1), I'm only 25. And (2), this writing stuff is really not my thing. I'm taking a stab at it since it runs in my blood. Well, my mom's blood. I figured since she does it maybe it would help me to try to do it too. To get the hurt and pain and anger out, you know what I'm sayin'? I haven't experienced a lot in my life, but the things that I have, that I remember, I'm putting it on paper. Why? Maybe, possibly, my life can

9

make an impact on someone else's life. Us young people gotta stick together 'cause with this generation death is all around us, you can even sniff it in the air. That's serious. God forbid if anything ever happened to me at least I feel like I'm leaving something positive behind. From that aspect it makes me feel pretty damned good.

Life was great. I had everything a child could ask for—a mother who did everything in her power to take care of my brother Anthony and me. My little brother made the sun shine with a crack of his smile. I was happy—couldn't ask for more. I remember the good days that might not seem like good days to someone else.

One day, my brother and I were at my dad's house. We were little around this time. Mom had taken us there since she had to talk to my dad. It was a sunny day in the summer. My uncle and aunt were home. I remember because they used to live downstairs. Mom headed upstairs to talk to dad. Anthony and I stayed outside playing in the dirt making mud pies. Lol.

It's kinda funny now that I'm thinking about it. Anthony and I were digging and digging with these tools and I happened to bend down at the wrong time. And BAM!

I felt this unbelievable pain in my head.

11

Anthony had hit me with a car jack. Yeah, he got me good, too. All I could see was all this blood running down my head and face. I hollered, cried, screamed. Man, I was soooo scared. Anthony didn't know what to do. Mom heard me screaming and came rushing downstairs. Her heart nearly stopped when she saw blood. She went nuts. She started screaming and yelling for my dad to hurry and come downstairs with a rag. The rag dad brought was a light color, but by the time he'd try to soak up the blood the rag was bloody red. Mom took over and applied pressure. I don't recall who called 911, if anyone did. Mom turned in Anthony's direction and had asked him, "Ant, what happened?" All he said was, "I didn't do it," all innocent and shit.

Okay. Now while all of this havoc was going on, I do remember now that my aunt and uncle called 911, so when the ambulance got to the house they rushed me to Wayne General Hospital in Wayne, New Jersey.

In the hospital I saw bright lights and lots of people sitting around me like crazy. I was scared out of my mind. Listen, the last time I'd been In the hospital was when I was little. I think I was dehydrating or something likes that. I remember being sick, real, real sick. And Mom took me to St. Joseph's Hospital, here in Paterson.

Once it was my turn to be seen I started biting my nails. I was so nervous. I remember the doctor had to stick a needle in my head. I remember getting stitches too. How many? That I don't remember. That was the first time I ever had stitches. After it was all said and done everyone was relieved, especially Anthony and me.

***

It was a nice summery day and Anthony and I were around the corner from our house at the park. There was a cookout going on at the house that was on the corner. And being that the park was right there we could see all these people in their backyard through the fence. They must've been all family. We didn't think anything of it because we had been playing in this park for years. Well, we were playing, alright.

13

We were swinging on the swings, sliding down the slides with the other kids. Then one of 'em started throwing rocks at my brother. So we started throwing rocks back at them. The way I looked at it everyone involved was about to get fucked up. If you mess with Anthony, you mess with me. It was going down! And down it went...

We got it popping!

Next thing we knew, we had the whole cookout on our asses. The kids' parents were trying to get at us. They were on it like they were going to kick our asses for real. Huh, they did not care that we were kids and that their children started it with us first. So they were popping all this shit, right. Saying what they were going to do to us. I was on it like FUCK that! So Anthony and I went and got my mom. Now let me describe mom. She was 5'4½" tall, slender and brown-skinned with long legs. She looked like a track runner. Mom looked like she couldn't harm a fly. That's what mom looked like, aiight. But looks can be deceiving.

Well, Mom walked around the corner with us and on the way we were explaining what

14

happened. But we kinda left out that it was a BIG ASS FAMILY (at least over 30 or so people or more) waiting. Lol.

Mom got up to the corner and saw all these people and all hell broke loose. The kids' parents started getting loud and popping shit to mom. So my MOTHER told them all to wait right there, she'll be rigggghhttttt back. Mom went home and got my aunt. Now let me describe aunty. Aunty was big-boned, need I say anymore. Oh man, my aunt was the wrong one to fuck wit'. My aunt didn't play that when it came to fucking with her sister or her nephews. Meanwhile, the people at the cookout were thinking mom was coming back with a lot of people. But they were in for the shock of their lives. Yep. It was just mom and my aunt and they were looking like, WHAT!!!

Someone in the crowd said, "They must be some bad bitches," because it was two against the whole cookout. My aunt and mom were ready to fight. Anthony and I were like, "We in there!" The way I looked at it was if we lose, huh, we lose as a family. Lol.

Well, things didn't go down. My mom and

this black lady ended up talking it out. On the way back home, mom was letting us know to stay out of trouble. That shit was crazy!

Now that I think about it...lol, lol, lol... laughing because I'm thinking about how us, four could have been fighting a whole cookout. Now that's what I call family time well spent.

***

I just thought of something reallllll crazy. I was at my dad's house on this particular day and I just knew that I was gonna die. No joke. See all of us, my dad, grandfather, grandmother, Anthony, my aunt, my other little brother T (on dad's side), and me were outside. So "my brothers", aunt, and I decided to get into this car my grandfather had in the driveway. Now mind you, this car had been there forever. I've never seen it moved. So we all climbed in the car and we were pretending it was ours. Now my aunt was in the driver's seat and we were in the passenger seat. I know you're wondering if my aunt was in the driver's seat, what was the problem then?

16

HOLD UP, I'm about to tell ya'll.

Well, my aunt was around my age. But back then I had to be like five or six years old and my aunt had to be just hitting high school. Anyway, my dad and grandfather were working on his truck that was sitting next to the car. My grandmother was sitting on the steps next to the car. So my aunt decided to pull the emergency brake, all of a sudden we all felt the car move. Everybody started jumping out and running. I wasn't so lucky to make it out in time.

The car had rolled back out into the street and I was hanging from the car door. I was screaming at the top of my lungs, HELP, HELP, HELLLLLLLLLLPPPPPPPPPP!!!!! I've never seen my father's eyes get so big before. I could tell that he was scared shitless. While I was hanging on the door the car was heading down the hill to oncoming traffic so without thinking my grandfather and dad jump into the truck that they were working on full speed ahead. They were trying to catch-up with the car. I was still hanging on for dear life, crying. They pulled up beside the car and my dad opened his door and reached out for me but he couldn't get close enough to grab me. I kept screaming HELP, HELP, HELLLLLLPPPPPPP! I was getting close to oncoming traffic so they tried it again but this time my dad was hanging from the truck and grabbed me. He threw me in the truck. Now the next problem was stopping the car before it caused a collision.

My grandfather drove even faster to get his truck in front of the car. Well, guess what he did it! I know you're reading this like yeah right that's some bullshit. But this is my life we are talking about here. Why would I lie? So finally once they got everything under control my dad steered the car backup to the house. Man, did they rip my aunt to shreds. All she could do was cry. And all I could do was thank God that I made it to see another day.

This may sound stupid to some but those were some of my good moments. After that nothing good happened. Life became a dreary tale, as you are about to read about. All I can tell you from this point on is to get some tissue 'cause it's going to be a tearjerker.

Things seemed to change as I aged over the years. What I mean is I started to notice certain things. Like how abusive my father was to my mom. For instance, how could he put his hands on the woman who gave his children life? Or how come he was never there for us when we needed him? He was *always* making promises that were never kept. I hated when he told my brother and me how he was coming to get us and never showed up. He'd have us sitting there waiting like jackasses.

Mom always told us to never get our hopes up 'cause he would just let us down. Man was she right! I guess the drugs were more important than the two boys he had waiting for him. What I didn't understand was after waiting around, when he finally did show up it was like nothing ever happened. That used to make me so mad. But at the end of the day, mom always came to save me. I loved her for that. She always tried to make light of a bad situation. But that isn't the half of it. Life became different especially after knowing that my dad wasn't worth two pennies rubbed together.

As time went on I started to notice something —see things on another level. Meaning I had to be the man of the house—protecting my

19

brother and mom. You see watching everything that was going on in the house; I started to notice something inside of me change. I had an angry side to me that would unleash. It first started when I went to school and I got jumped. My father told me if I came home and let somebody else whoop my ass he was going to whoop my ass. Those words stuck with me for the rest of my life. I started fighting—getting into trouble all 'cause I was scared to get my ass whooped. At the same time I also noticed that I was turning into him.

Mom also told me never to be like my father —to have my own identity. Honestly, I didn't know who I was. But in a lot of ways I was just like *him*. This goes back to what I was saying that the beast was about to be unleashed.

I felt like a pit bull that was in attack mode. I couldn't control it all because of that father of mine. You know how they say a good thing gone bad. That was me.

My father turned me into a monster. And the person who dealt with it was mom, which I felt was pretty messed up on his part because he needed to be there to put me in my place.

Instead he left everything on *her*. And till this day I don't know how she did it.

Mom was more of a father to me than my own dad. I started to wonder maybe my brother and I did something wrong for dad not to be there. Dad had a new family and basically said screw us. That crushed me being the first-born. Wondering would I ever have a father who would want to actually be a father —a father who would play with us, take us out to the park—just anything to show us that he cared and not leave so much pressure on my mom. Again, the beast was burning inside. And I didn't know what to do to control it. I thought that was bad, but what was coming next was worse.

Nothing could prepare any of us for what was waiting down this dark winding road.

***

Ant got sick. My brother and I were always together, except in school. I never noticed any change in him. Ant was a six-year old playful and happy kid. We played everyday, watched

Power Rangers together. Mom didn't even notice it, not until she got that phone call saying that Ant was falling asleep in class. That was weird 'cause Ant loved school. He was also an honor roll student. So when we heard that it threw us for a loop. So mom took him to the doctor and that's when my life took a turn in a different direction.

Ant had a brain tumor called some big ass word. Holdup, um, ah, ah...(wait a minute lemme ask my mom) oh, it's called Glioblastoma. If anyone would have told us this was going to happen I would've called them a friggin' liar. As I recollect (closing my eyes) everything happened something like this:

February 3, 1995

St. Joseph's Hospital was where the first surgery was performed. For that moment I felt a world of happiness on my mom and my face because the surgery was a success. Of course Ant was not totally out of the woods, but he was still alive and that was a blessing to us. Everything was fine. But then, two month's later the tumor came back. Another surgery was performed. And the tumor came back in two weeks. That's when the *beast* unleashed in me.

Ant got sicker and sicker. He started losing weight, sleeping way too much, not wanting to eat, losing his hair, couldn't walk on his own, use the bathroom by himself. This was not my brother! The cancer was taking over.

Mom was doing her best to take care of him —taking Ant to his doctor appointments. Making sure he ate, doing her motherly duties. Me, on the other hand, I could only do so much, but I was there. We both took turns taking care of him, but mom mostly ran herself crazy running to and from St. Joseph's Hospital as well as Hackensack University Medical Center, but we managed to do things as a family. What other choices did we really have?

Sitting back watching all this just tore me up inside. I was watching my brother suffer. There was nothing I could do to save him. He was dying right in front of me. Ant went blind, couldn't walk, and nothing they did at the hospital helped. The cancer was winning and I was furious! Going to the hospital to visit Ant just made things worse for me 'cause I couldn't play or doing any of the things we used to do together. My anger skyrocketed and the demon in me erupted in ways you couldn't even imagine.

Dad still wasn't around. This was the time mom, Ant, and I needed him the most. Again, he let us down. This made me hate him. I was like, "FUCK that nigga! He ain't shit to me!" Like always mom was the strong one and I looked up to her.

During all of this, Ant didn't want to stay in the hospital anymore so he asked could he come home. Ant came home along with his hospital bed and meds. Ant stayed in mom's bedroom and we took care of him there. I felt like we were a family again.

Taking care of him was hard on my mother and me but we stayed on top of it. It was a 24/7 job taking care of one another. The thing that killed me most was that my father finally started popping up. Finally, he saw for himself what the hell was going on with his son. I didn't know if it finally hit that we needed him around, but after a while I suddenly didn't care. All I could think about was whooping his ass.

During this time, Dad started coming around more often but something wasn't right. We finally found out what that was. My father was plotting to steal my brother's meds. Now this just made me want to kill the man that helped put me on this earth. How can you come around after all this and think to steal from your own son? It was bad enough that he stole from him out of the hospital. My uncle T had given Anthony a wallet with five dollars in it. Ant had the wallet in a drawer in his room and dad had come to visit that day. Mom was already there, but she left because she was exhausted. By the time mom got home she realized that she had forgotten the five dollars in the wallet. Come the next day, mom rushed to get to the hospital and checked the drawer only to find the wallet there but the five dollars was gone. Dad had taken it.

After all the *shit* mom and I went through to make sure Ant was healthy. Dad was being selfish worrying about himself and his habit. I was beyond livid. If there weren't so many laws,

God only knows. This also made mom angry too so she kicked him out and told him to never return.

Around this time, I was attending Public School No. 5 and trying not to think about what was going on at home. That didn't work.

I was in class just like any other day. I went to the YMCA after school program like I normally did. The thing that seemed weird was that mom wasn't the one who came to pick me up. It was my Aunt Lee. I asked my aunt where mom was and she wouldn't answer me, not at first. Finally, she told me mom was home. We got to the house and there were so many people at my house. I figured we were having a party. That was until I got upstairs. My brother was lying in his hospital bed in mom's bedroom and there were family, friends, and some acquaintances surrounding him. It was November 2, 1995. I will never forget this day. It's like a movie in my head.

I remember feeling numb watching two young men dressed in business suits from Bragg Funeral Home put my skeletal-formed brother in a black body bag. I watched with anguish in my eyes them carefully place his emaciated body in the back of their van and drive off. It didn't hit me right then and there that he was never coming back. I was nine, and oblivious of what death really meant. I had no idea that it meant permanent. That was the first time I felt myself die inside. I was alone. I watched them take my brother away from me and put him in a *black body bag*. I can't seem to get the image out of my head. That made me so fuckin' mad. I was more hurt than anything mainly because I never got a chance to properly say… *goodbye*. Ant was seven years old when he died. And I was nine—nine and on the verge of having a nervous breakdown. Being a kid seemed so unfair especially when your life was being cut short.

On top to this, my father left me right after my brother's funeral. So I lost my brother and my father in the same month. How messed up was that! Still in all moms was there.

After all of this had happened I noticed that the demon inside of me had finally taken over. I became evil. I blamed my mom for everything that had happened. Reason being I never really talked about how I was feeling. Hell, I didn't even cry looking at my brother the night that he had passed. So all that anger that I was feeling came out at my mom 'cause she was the only one I had left. I took her for granted; yet she never left my side. She always hung in there with me and sometimes I wonder why.

I was fist fighting my mom. We would yell at each other—never saw things eye-to-eye. I noticed we weren't the same people anymore. We didn't hangout anymore. Talk or just be around each other. I was home a lot by myself after my brother died. I needed someone to talk to. I didn't have that and being that it was crazy at the house I turned to the streets and found my "new brothers", which were Playa, Greedy, Phat, Deal, Ice-Pic, GU, Chain and M-Dot. They could never replace Ant, but it was a start. I looked at the streets as my FATHER. The streets taught me a lot. Things he didn't as well as things he couldn't because he was too busy getting high. Drugs numbed him and in some ways me too.

That's when the girls came into the picture. That was my way of having a woman around 'cause my mother wasn't home. No woman could replace my mom but I needed that female around when mom wasn't. At the same time of needing a female I was also chillin' wit' my new brothers and that changed who I was. I started drinking, smoking, and having sex. I was completely out of control.

See smoking weed was the best thing that could have happened to me. It was my getaway. Weed took me to places where I wouldn't have to think about my brother's death. But over time, smoking didn't help. The memories played over and over again in my head. Also, things with mom were still crazy, but being with my boys made things a little easy.

By this time, the kids were bulling me in my school so mom somehow got me transferred to Norman S. Weir to stop me from fighting about the death of my brother. Yeah, kids can be cruel.

I just finished with grammar school and on my way to high school. Good ole' John F. Kennedy. Man, I couldn't wait to get there, but once I got there, I couldn't stay in class...*too* busy chasing those girls...too busy fighting, just doin' whatever I felt like doing. You know a lot of shit changed. I started noticing that I just didn't care about anything anymore, not even myself.

As time went on I started hanging in the streets more and more. Chillin' wit' "my brothers" were the only things that made sense to me. Things at the house were still fucked up; reason being my grandfather was selling the house. Of course this shit made my mom and I even more pissed off.

***

CHECK HOW THIS WENT DOWN...

My brother just died, father just left, now we had to find somewhere else to live. The fucked up part of this was on some short notice bullshit. So you know I was beyond PISSED! I had to leave everything I knew. Paterson was everything to me. North 7th Street was my 'hood and I loved it. So when mom came to me and told me it was time to go, I was not trying to hear that shit. But around that age I had no choice. When you look at it I had no one but my mom *sooooooo* mom came wit' the U-haul truck, and all I could think about was having to start all over again— making new friends, new school, new everything. I was not happy. And out of all of this I had to leave my brother Ant.

All the memories of me and my brother playing in the park, watching TV, playing with toys in the backroom, doing homework together, going out with mom—it all hit me at once and it wasn't shit I could do. I felt helpless. So after I realized that my life was about to change again, mom told me to get in the truck, we had to leave.

I didn't know where we were going or what to expect. All I knew was that I didn't want to go. So finally, we moved to Clifton, New Jersey, and once we got settled there I passed out on my bed. Guess mom was looking at it as a new beginning and I was looking at it, as I just didn't want to be there.

So the next day, I woke up and shit wasn't the same right away. What I mean was that it was a whole new environment: green grass that was well manicured. Birds were singing. The area in which we lived was clean. Even the air smelled different. With all of that I *still* wasn't happy. I missed bottles breaking, cops sirens, people yelling, but the biggest thing I missed was "my brothers". That same day I wanted to go back home. Back to Paterson, so I called my nigga and was ready to make the trip back to the 'hood. Mom was not trying to hear that! We ended up getting into a big ass argument. I ended up walking all the way from Clifton to Paterson.

Once I got to Paterson, I was so happy to see my boys. Meanwhile, mom and me were still going through it, so I stayed in Paterson and didn't go back home for about two days. Wasn't even thinking about Clifton I was just happy to be home.

During this time mom was looking all over for me. It got so bad that she had to report me *missing*. Now mind you, I knew nothing about this. Finally, I decided to go home so I walked back to Clifton, not knowing what waited for me once I got there. Well, once I got home mom was so worried. I knew she was sad because her eyes said it all...red puffy swollen eyes, yeah, that look of her crying herself sick. It brought me back to when mom had wrote this poem about me called I Just Died...

I just died when the phone rang
The police office stated his name,
The crackle in his voice made an eyebrow rise
He asked if I was the mother in the house
If not, was it possible to speak to my spouse?
I'm a single mother
Who carried the burdens alone

The office asked that I come down to the morgue,
To identify the unknown deceased,
Since my child too, was reported missing,
I felt the need to oblige.
I entered the cold, lifeless room,
Inside I cried.
Outside I sighed with relief,
As the young man was unknown to me
Death met by a bullet lodged in his brain.
I prayed silently for his mom and dad,
How sad to be called to identify your child,
I grieved myself and went back home.
To an empty house

Two days later I received another call,
The police officer stated his name,
The crackle in his voice made an eyebrow rise,
By now he was familiar to me,

Knowing I am a single mother and all,
He advised me to come down to the morgue,
To identify the unknown deceased,
I pleaded, "Please, Lord, don't let it be!"
I entered the cold, lifeless room
It had a stench that sickened me,
Within my gut I felt something was wrong,
A second passed before I could see,
I was startled by the view of my child,
Laid motionless there on the stretcher,
With a stab wound deep in his chest,
I hollered in anguish
My child died before me!
That's not how its'sposed to be!
Why is this happening to me?"
Hysterical, I screamed at the top of my lungs,
Lord, how come you allowed this to be?
Why my child?
Answer me!!!!!
I stood there grieving angrily,
Waiting for His response,
Each night I wait,
Each day I wait for Him to come and talk,
The walls are silent in my home,
But a beam of light shines through,
It let's me know I am not alone,
My son's memory is with me,
I look up at the ceiling,
I praise the Lord for forgiving me
For my shortsightedness,
I thought I had died when I viewed my son,
But now I can see I live,
I'll meet 'em both at the Golden Gates.
—*Karla Denise Baker*

The doorbell rang. It was the cops and they sat me down and explained to me the dos and don'ts of being an out-of-control adolescent.

Well, after that crazy weekend it was time to deal wit' school. Clifton High School was something I was not ready for and I was something Clifton High was not ready for either. The first year was ok, I met new people. I got through it with no problem. Now, the second year, I couldn't say that because I started meeting the females all hell broke loose. I started doing things like cutting class, chillin' wit' those girls, and having sex without a care in the world. Staying out all times of the night, leaving the house, cutting school whenever I wanted to, getting suspended like crazy, and of course my grades dropped, bringing girls to my house and doin' the do, smoking weed hea-vy and drinking. Even outside of school girls were on my mind. You see I started traveling going to Rahway, Essex County, Nutley, Wallington, Passaic and Garfield. Mom always told me to stop chasing those fast ass girls. Well, I never listened and it finally caught up with me.

One day, I decided to bring a girl to my house. No need to tell you what happened. Just use your head. Mom was at work. Well, anyway, the next morning the girl and her parents came to my house. Let me tell you her father wasn't happy. He was on it like he was going to take me to jail. What was a nigga to do? I was out of control without a care in the world. For instance, if I remember correctly, I just had got out of some other shit a couple of day's prior. Now what had happened was I was hanging out wit' a girl of mine. Mom was out with her girlfriend and I had just gotten home. So I made the choice to sneak back out. If I knew what I knew today I would've stayed home. But I didn't and I ended up going to the Clifton jail that night. I let my anger get the best of me because when I got home, mom was already home and locked me out. Mom questioned me through the door and I snapped. I started kicking the door in. My anger was in the highs. I became the BEAST. It seemed like no matter what I did nothing mattered to me. Nothing mattered until my freedom was nearly taken from me. Once I was released from the holding cell, not too long after that things returned back to the same ole' shit again.

My senior year, mom was happy but I managed to screwed things up again. I ended up getting left back. For one, I never liked to take gym. How could I flunk gym? Easy. I was too busy running the streets. The streets had a hold on me—a hold that couldn't be broken. So knowing what I knew I said, "Fuck school!" See the way I saw it I had another year to do, so why bother to go to class. Mom used to always tell me, "If you keep playin' around life will pass you by." Boy was she telling me the damn truth.

Day by day, I started to see mom giving up on me. Friends' started to stray and I started to lose everything. Sooooo my second year as a senior came and I had a different attitude. Or so I thought. What I mean is things were going good. My grades were better. I actually stayed in class. But then, I noticed old habits die-hard. I started cutting and doing me again.

Now why was I cutting class? I met a girl that I had never met before in Clifton. She had looks, style, and attitude—everything I was looking for. Her name was Naomi and she was that "*bitch*." We did everything together: smoked weed, drink, talked on the phone, chilled every day.

Anything you could think of we did. I was in love.

Now pay close attention because this is where shit got crazy.

During this time I was still fuckin' up in school. I ended up getting into a fight that got me suspended for 42 days. Like I said in the beginning there was a demon inside of me. Now during my "vacation" I was getting phone calls like crazy that stated that Naomi was cheating on me with other niggas I knew. She was just doin' her. That shit just fucked me up even more. On top of that shit I was fucked at home because mom was on the verge of losing the apartment, so for me to clear my mind I got high to take the pain that I was feeling away.

Once I got back to school that next day I ended up getting kicked out of Clifton High, too busy fucking around, wasting time fucking around. The funny part was that I only needed 5 credits to graduate. Now that same day I saw Naomi and confronted her about what was said about her cheating on me with other niggas. She told me it was all a lie, but for some reason I didn't believe her. A person's eyes tell a lot, but that was the least of my worries. My biggest worry was how I was going to tell my mom I had just gotten kicked out of school. Well, to my surprise, my mom was four-steps ahead of me. She already knew and man was she heated. I was scared for my life and if I didn't know any better I thought she was going to have my head for dinner. Now this didn't make shit easier for mom. Hell, we never had it easy.

So later that day, I was sitting in my room saying to myself I was officially a *bum*. No diploma, no job, not a pot to piss in. A year went by and shit was still fucked up. Mom was trying to figure out what to do with me because she couldn't keep up with the rent as well as my many mistakes. We were about to be homeless!

Mom couldn't send me to my father because I was better off in hell. She tried sending me to her brother, but they barely spoke. Nah, I wasn't having that. How you gonna send me to someone who doesn't even speak to you, huh? You feel me? Exactly.

I ended up taking night classes trying to get my GED, but that didn't work out. So mom came up with the idea of sending me to Job Corp. That way I could getaway from the bullshit, learn some discipline, learn a trade, and get myself together and protect me so that I wouldn't be on the streets. Job Corp was a place where they gave you room and board. Plus they gave you an education. So off to Job Corp I went, while mom tried to get things back on track.

Now things kinda fucked me up while I was in Job Corp because I fought like I was locked up in jail. The only good thing about Job Corp was that they had girls in there, other than that; Job Corp was like being imprisoned. I mean you had to get up early, eat, shower, and go to bed when *they* told you to. On top of that niggas was getting their ass kicked while they were asleep. Niggas were robbing people, smoking weed, drinking, FUCK…you name it. Everything mom tried to get me away from was there behind closed doors. I was miserable.

After a while I noticed I had reverted back to the same shit. I started smoking weed, drinking, having sex with girls anywhere on campus. Shit was crazy. Crazy niggas started bringing guns.

They damn near beat this kid to death. I had to get the fuck outta there, but I had nowhere to go so I had no choice but to stay.

One day, while I was in my trade class, which was brick masonry; I got hit in the face with a brick. Man, I went straight 'hood on that nigga. Once I was through wit' him he knew that I was from Paterson. I didn't go to Job Corp to fight, I went there to learn but I had no choice but to defend myself. It seemed like no matter where I was trouble was right behind me.

A couple of days later I got into another fight, which led to me getting kicked out of Job Corp. Well, once again I was on the move again...back home. Or so I thought. I had three suitcases as I boarded the train back to Clifton.

Once I got home, mom had already lost the apartment. The rent was $894 plus the electric and she couldn't handle it alone. I believe her unemployment had run out and she didn't find another job right away. She was dating some dude, but he had his own baggage (that she'll have to fill you in on).

Anyway, I didn't know where mom was. She didn't know that I had gotten kicked out either.

41

Finally, I got back to my 'hood of Paterson and my boys came to get me. Now mind you, I didn't have anywhere's to live and I only had $25.00 dollars to my name, so my boy said that I could stay wit' him for a little while, but he was still living home wit' his parents. His parents didn't know I was staying there until later. Well, that same day and I bumped into an old friend who told me that my girl Naomi was having a baby by another man.

Now check this…

While I was in Job Corp, Naomi and I talked every day. She never told me about this new nigga. I even saw her when I would come home on the weekends. That shit fucked me up and for the first time I had my heartbroken. Never knew what that felt like but that day it hit home. While all of this was going on I bumped into someone who knew where my mom was. I told them to tell her I was home and that I had nowhere to go. Yeah, I was officially homeless. Finally, my mom and I reached each other and I told her everything. Where she was staying I couldn't go. I was like damn things couldn't get any worse. Oh, my bad, I was wrong…I forgot to tell you that I ended up getting kicked out of my boy's house too. His parents said that I couldn't stay wit' them. So I ended up staying at my other boy's house. I was there for a while. For the time that I was there I was looking for a job, but no one would hire me because I had no high school diploma or GED. So then his father said I couldn't stay there any more either. I was shit out of luck: no job, no schooling, and no home. My palms balled, temples throbbed, heart raced, eyes drooped…"the BEAST"… had unleashed. WHAT DA FUCK!!!!

No doubt my mom was steamed! So she came up wit' an idea that I stay at my grandmother's house. Now things got crazier once I got there because my grandmother was already crazy in the head. She suffered from schizophrenia and that shit was no joke for someone who was not used to it. I still didn't have any money. I couldn't help my grandmother or myself. I had no choice but to depend on my mom for money. I got tired of asking her for money. I was thinking of other ways to get money so I started looking for a job. But no jobs called me for an interview. I got tired of being broke so I started selling drugs to survive. The money was coming in like wildfire and I was able to eat.

During this time I was still looking for a job. One day, at my boy's house he told me about this school he went to, called, um, ah, ah, oh yeah... New Jersey Youth Corp. He said it was a good school and that I should check it out. Now if you remember in the beginning I told you I only needed 5 credits to graduate if I had stayed in Clifton High. Well, I decided to go back to school. Once I made that decision I left the drug game alone and got a JOB.

A lot of things started to hit me and I started looking at the bigger picture. I worked from 10 p.m. to 6 a.m. and went to school straight after work. It was a lot on me but I was damn sure going to make sure I got that paper. On the other hand things didn't work out wit' the job. It was just too much so I stopped and focused on school. I got my diploma! Man, oh man, did that feel great! It was the proudest moment I have ever experienced in my entire life. Mom couldn't stop smiling. She finally got to see me walk the stage. Yeah, things were finally coming together for me and I started to see that life is what you make it.

After I received my diploma I got a full-time job working at a food market in Ridgewood, New Jersey. I worked my butt off. I worked there for a year and a half and then got a promotion as a supervisor. I got my own apartment at 23. I was doing great! But sometimes life takes one down a detour that they never see coming. What I mean is I was terminated from my job after 2 years of backbreaking service. I let my apartment go because trying to pay for rent was killing my pockets, not to mention I had other things that had to be taken cared of like: food, laundry, haircut, train ticket. A nigga had to keep himself as well as his gear tight; you know what I'm sayin'?

I guess you're wondering what I am up to now. Well, I still live in Paterson. I'm trying to bounce back. Things are not the best wit' this recession an all but I will not stop until I am back on top again. 'Ey, if I did it once I know that I can do it again. Yeah, I got mad confidence as well as inspiration from my mom. Man, listen, I don't know how she does it and still manages to look like my sister. Lol.

HOLD UP!!!!!!

"There goes my ba-by..." Ah shit! Usher done started something here. Damn, she's finneeeee!

Oh see, ya'll gonna have to wait 'cause I'm about to get my MAC on....

To be continued...

Epilogue

Now I wrote this book not so people could just know a little about my life. Look, I'm only twenty-five I still have a lot of living to do. I wrote this book so that I could possibly help some young person my age. No matter what you go through keep fighting with your mind instead of your fists. Be thankful for what you have. If you have a parent that has been there for you through hell and back forgive the ones you feel fucked up your life. Show them the love they deserve. Don't let this world eat you whole. If you don't believe what I am saying just look at me.

I am a fighter and always will be. There's no telling what you can do, but you have to want it that badly. Don't let anything stop you and keep your head held high. Push yourself, and most importantly stay in school and if you are not in school go back to school. Knowledge is power. And the POWER in these streets, I hate to say it is DEATH. Find yourself. Yeah, find yourself 'cause dealing wit' the shit us young people are currently going through ain't no joke. Often I felt

47

like I'd rather be dead than to deal wit' this shit. But I stopped tripping and starting using this head that is attached to my shoulders. Yo, LIFE is what you make it. So the struggle continues...

Peace, Love, & Life

Craig

Acknowledgments

To God, for giving me the life I have lived.

To Mom, thanks for helping me and guiding me through life as a strong black woman.

To my woman, Miah, I thank you for being my friend, wonderful woman, and for standing behind me during the rough times.

To Phat, thanks for being my boy.

To Me, (not to sound conceited), for believing in myself enough to write this book.

To my brother, Anthony, for being my brother and making this book possible.

To New Jersey Youth Corp., for teaching me that there are people who see things in you that you never see in yourself.

To Dad, I thank you for teaching me to be my own man. I realize that I am not you.

And lastly, I thank the Streets, for teaching me that I deserved so much more than jail, drugs, or death.